Helen Leigh

Miscellaneous Poems

Helen Leigh

Miscellaneous Poems

ISBN/EAN: 9783744713184

Printed in Europe, USA, Canada, Australia, Japan

Cover: Foto ©Thomas Meinert / pixelio.de

More available books at **www.hansebooks.com**

MISCELLANEOUS POEMS.

MISCELLANEOUS POEMS,

BY

HELEN LEIGH,

OF

MIDDLEWICH.

MANCHESTER:
PRINTED BY C. WHEELER,
AND SOLD BY MESS. CLARKES, BOOKSELLERS, IN THE MARKET-PLACE.
M,DCC,LXXXVIII.

TO

THOMAS WILLIS, Esq.

THE FOLLOWING

POEMS

ARE,

BY PERMISSION,

WITH HUMBLE RESPECT AND GRATITUDE,

INSCRIBED;

BY

HIS MOST OBEDIENT,

AND OBLIGED SERVANT,

HELEN LEIGH.

PREFACE.

THOUGH an Apology is undoubtedly requisite for the Publication of the following Sheets, I must confess that I have, in Reality, no *plausible* one to make, if declaring myself the Wife of a Country Curate, and Mother of seven Children, will not be deemed sufficient.

My most grateful Acknowledgments are due to those Ladies and Gentlemen who have so generously patronized this Work; and shall ever remain

        Their most obliged

            Humble Servant,

                H. LEIGH.

A LIST of the SUBSCRIBERS.

A.

MISS S. Antrobus, *Knutsford*
   Mr. Antrobus, *Macclesfield*
Mr. J. Antrobus, *Manchester*
   Antrobus, *Congleton*
Rev. Mr. Atkinson, *Leek*
Mr. Alcock, *Sandbath*
W. Afton, *Northwich*
Shaw Allanson, *Haydock*
Arrowsmith, *Kermincham*
T. Ashcroft, *Prescot*
J. Astley, *London*
M. Amson, *Over-Peever*
Aldcroft, *Manchester*
T. Ashton, *ditto*
Allen, *Macclesfield*
F. Ashley, *Frodsham*
Mrs. Alsager, *Congleton*
Mr. G. Alexander, *Acton*
Mrs. Astle, *Chester*

B.

J. H. Smith Barry, *Belmount*, 4 copies
Miss Barry, 2 copies
W. E. Bootle, Esq. *Latham*
A. Bracebridge, Esq. *Brereton*, 2 copies
Rev. Mr Booth, *Twemlow*, 5 copies
Mrs. Booth, 5 copies
R. Barnston, Esq. *Chester*, 2 copies
S. Bower, Esq. *Altringham*
J. Bower, Esq *Gross-lane*
J. Blackburn, Esq. *Hale*

Rev. T. Blackburn, *Thelwall*, 2 copies
S. Barrow, Esq. *Nantwich*
Miss Blackburn, *Liverpool*
J. Bailey, Esq. *Sandbach*
Mr. Barrow, *Sedburgh*
   Booth, *Congleton*
S. Beckett, *Middlewich*
T. Beckett, *ditto*
J. Brown, *Prescot*
D. Backhouse, *Liverpool*
Mrs Brown, *Middlewich*
Mr. Bunall, *ditto*
P. Bradburn, *Northwich*
W. Bradburn *ditto*
T. Barrett, *Stroud*
Boyer, *Northwich*
T. J. Brayne, *ditto*, 2 copies
Rev. Mr. Brayshav, *Davenham*
   Mr. Birch, *Great Budworth*
Mr. T. Bull, *Sandbach*
P. Banner, *Great Budworth*
W. Butters *Rudheath*
R. Brady, *Northwich*
N. Beaman, *ditto*
   Burgess, *ditto*
Rev. Mr. Burrows, *Goostry*
Rev. Mr. Baldwin, *Northwich*
Mrs. Bayles, *Derby*
Mr. Bartlett, *Knutsford*
   Billingham, *ditto*
J. Bakewell, *Chester*
   Barnett, *Swettenham*
J Bostock, *ditto*
J. Bailey, *Midglereck*

(2)

Mr. A. Bailey, *Midgbrook*
Boydell, *Middlewich*
J. Bloor, *Liverpool*
R. Barford, *ditto*
R. Brooke, *ditto*
Mrs. Richmond, *ditto*
Miss Briggs, *Chester*
Mrs. Beresford, *Ashbourn*
F. Beresford, *ditto*
W. Beresford, *ditto*
Biddleston, *ditto*
Mr. C. Buchanan, *Frodsham*
L. Bleale, *ditto*
J Booth, *Somerford*
Batterfbee, *Manchester*
R. Buckey, *ditto*
Banks, Lecturer in Philosophy,
Mrs. Banks
Mr. J. Bancroft, *ditto*
Berry, *ditto*
Rev. J. Brookes, *ditto*
Mr. E. Barlow, *ditto*
B. Barlow, *ditto*
J. Barton, *ditto*
H. Barton, *ditto*
G. Barton, *ditto*
J. Booth, *ditto*
S. Birch, *ditto*
Mrs. Burchell, *ditto*
Rev. T Barnes, D. D. *ditto*
Rev. Mr. Bradbury. *ditto*
Mr. A. Birch, *Ardewick*
Barnett, *Middlewich*
C. Bate, *Nantwich*
Beswick, *Macclesfield*
Brandreth, *Buxton*
Mrs. Bates, *ditto*
Mr. Blackey, *ditto*
Buckley, *Biley*
S Bailey, *Knutsford*
A. Becket, *Arley*
Bafnett, *Croxton*
T. Brise II, *Minshull*
Rev. Mr. Baldwin. *Leyland*
Mr. Barnston, *Chester*
Miss Bowcock, *ditto*
Mr. J. Bailey, *ditto*
Boulper, *ditto*
W. Brown, *ditto*
R. Bowers, *ditto*
Rev. Mr. Bateman. *Sedbergh*
Captain Bennett, *Chester*

Rev. T. Broadhurst, *Chester*
Mr. A. Berks, *ditto*
Boyer, *ditto*
Rev. Mr. Bennett, *Manchester*
Mr. W Bilsborough, *ditto*
H. Bell, *Prescot*
G. La Bruyere, *ditto*
F. Boult, *Chester*
J. Brown, *Liverpool*

C.

R. Cumberbach, Esq. *Congleton*
Miss Cumberbach, *ditto*
W. F. B. Cloughton, Esq. *Claughton*
J. Cheshire, Esq. *Hartford*
— Gamplin, Esq. *Liverpool*
Mr. Camplin
Doctor Currie. *Chester*
Mr. Clubbe, *Congleton*, 2 copies
Mrs. Collier, *ditto*
Mr. Copeland, *ditto*
Cotgrave, *Torwin*
Cartwright *Stantborn*
Miss Croxton, *Middlewich*
Mr. G. Chesworth, *ditto*
J. Carter, *ditto*
Cooper, *Sandbach*
J. W. Clofe, *Liverpool*
Rev. T. Clarkson, *London*
Mr. Chalinor, *Leek*
Mrs. Chalinor
Crusoe, *ditto*
Mr. Chandley. *Warrington*
Miss Corles, *Chester*
Mr. F. Clayton, *ditto*
J. Cattrall. *Charnock*
Rev. Mr. Coman, *Mobberley*
Mr. T. Chantler, *Northwich*
Colville, *ditto*
Mrs. Carter, *ditto*
Mr. J. Carter, *ditto*
W. Crofs, *Nantwich*
Cowper, *Knutsford*
Rev. Mr. Clowes, *Manchester*
Mr. Crompton, *ditto*
R. Chambers, *ditto*
W. Chesworth, *ditto*
I. Cowgill, *ditto*
H. Carke, *ditto*
Miss Cochran, *Wigan*
Mr. T. Copeland, *London*

(3)

Mr. B Cook, *Manchester*
T. Cheshire, at *Lodge*, near *Hatton*, *Cheshire*

D.

T. Dixon, Esq. *Chester*
P. Downes, Esq *Butley*
Mr. Downes, *Manchester*
Rev. Mr. Davies, *Macclesfield*
Mr. E. Davies, *Chester*
Miss Daintry, *Macclesfield*
Mr. R. Deane, *ditto*
W. Deane, *Midalewich*
Dean, *Congleton*
C. Dodd, *Macclesfield*
Dodson, *ditto*
D Dale, *Liverpool*
Dawson, *Sedburgh*
J. Dennel, *Chester*
Davenport, *ditto*
J. Davenport, *Acton*
C. Davenport, *Nantwich*
Mr R. Daxon, *Warrington*
E Dakin, *ditto*
Dawson, *Northwich*
J. Dunn, *ditto*
J Darlington, *Middlewich*
G. Darlington, *Davenham*
T. Darcy, *Morton*
J. Douglass, *Birmingham*
Mrs. Dickenson, *Tarvin*
Mrs. Dixon, *Manchester*
Mr. J. Doxon, *ditto*
Miss J. Dodson, *Northwich*
Mr. Dean, *London*, 2 copies
T. Darlington, *Reddish*
J. Dickenson, *Middlewich*

E.

Mrs. Egerton, *Oulton*, 2 copies
Mrs. Egerton, *Chester*
P Ellames Esq *ditto*
J. Eaton, Esq. *Crosby*
Rev. Mr. Eaton. *Chester*
R. Earl, Esq. *Liverpool*
Mr Earl *Overton*
Rev. C. Etheliton, *Manchester*
Mr. Ellis, *Chester*

Mr. R. Eyres, *Middlewich*
Miss M. Edge, *Northwich*
Mr. Evans, *Knutsford*
J. Entwisle, *Manchester*

F.

T. Faulkner, Esq. *Chester*, 2 copies
—— Fosbrooke, Esq. *ditto*
Mrs Fosbrooke
C. Ford, Esq. *Manchester*
Rev Guy Fairfax, *Wigan*
Capt. Furnivall, *Sanabach*
Mr. G. Furnivall, *ditto*
Furey, *Winnington*
J. Fletcher, *Warrington*
Mrs. Fox, *Davenport*
Mr. Freeman, *Chester*
Forbes, *ditto*
J. Fluitt, *Chester*
Foden, *Knutsford*
Foden, *Brereton*
T. Foden, *Withington*
Foden, *Manchester*
Filkin, *Northwich*
T. Filkin, *ditto*
Mrs. Formoston, *ditto*
Mr. T. Farrell, *Frodsham*
Falkner, *Barton*
S. Falkner, *Manchester*
T. M. Froggatt, *ditto*
R. Forrester, *ditto*
J. Foster, *ditto*
Fisher, *ditto*
J. Fidlin, *ditto*

G.

Honourable Booth Grey, *Wincham*, 2 copies
Honourable John Grey, *Chester*, 2 copies
Honourable Mrs. John Grey, 2 copies
John Clegg, Esq. *Withington*
L. P. Grayson, Esq. *Liverpool*
Rev. M. Griffith, D. D. *Manchester*
Rev. J. Griffith, A. M. *Blakeley*
Mrs. Gawthrop, *Sedburgh*
Rev. G. Gardner, *Chester*
Mr J. Gardner, *Nantwich*
Miss Garrick, *Weaverham*

(4)

Rev. Mr. Gatley, *Knutsford*
Mr. Galley, *Sandbach*
Goodwin, *Buxton*
S. Goodwin, *Macclesfield*
J. Goff, *Swettenham*
Captain Gibbons, *Liverpool*
Mr. Greaves, *Bakewell*
Mrs. Garle, *Ashbourn*
Mr. Gorton, *Salford*
J. Godfrey, *Manchester*
J. Grime, *ditto*

H.

Henry Hesketh, Esq. *Chester*
H. Hayward, Esq. *ditto*
Doctor Haygarth, *ditto*
Rev. Mr. Hodgrs, *Holmes Chapel*
Mrs. Heyes, *Sedbergh*
Rev. Mr. Hunter, *Weaverham*
Mrs. Harding, *Newton*
Mr. R. Huxley, *Bradford*
Mr. Henderson, *Middlewich*, 2 copies
Hare, *ditto*
Hope, *Stockport*, 4 copies
Hopley, *Occlestone*
Mrs. Howard, *Hulmalfield*
Mr. P. Hankinson, *Warrington*
T. Horner, *ditto*
Hostage, *Chester*
Hallwood, *ditto*
Miss Harwood, *ditto*
Mr. Harding, *Liverpool*
J. Hitchin, *ditto*
T. Hardy, *ditto*
Rev. Mr. Hodson, *ditto*
Mr. Hill, *Chester*
Harrop, *ditto*
Hilditch, *Moss-end*
P. Hilditch, *Nantwich*
J. Hilditch, *Bletchton*
W. Hilditch, *Wheelock*
P. Hardy, *London*
G. Holland, *Middlewich*
L. Hall, *ditto*
Hewson, *ditto*
M. Hudson, *ditto*
Hudson, *Macclesfield*
Harper, *Petty Wood*
S. Hares, *Acton*
Harrison, *Sandbach*
Rev. J. Harrison, *Overton*

Mrs. Harrison
Mr. Harrison
Hulse, *Croxton*
Hargreave, *Leek*
Harwar, *Congleton*
Rev. Mr. Hatton, *Lymm*
Rev. Mr. Hervey, *Caldon*
Rev. Mr. Hornby, *Wimwick*, 2 copies
Miss P. Hale, *Darnhall*
Mr. Hunt, *Northwich*
J. Hunt, *ditto*
D. Hall, *Macclesfield*
Hawkins, *ditto*
T. Hall, *ditto*
S. Haslehurst, *ditto*
Hadfield, *ditto*
Miss Hordern, *ditto*
Mr. Hale, *ditto*
J. Hollins, *Knutsford*
W. Hollins, *ditto*
Holland, *ditto*
Hancock, *ditto*
Howard, *ditto*
Mrs. Hodgson, *Congleton*
Mrs. Hodgson, *Ashbourn*
Miss Hodgson, *Crakemass*
Mr. R. Hodgson, *Congleton*
J. Hodgson, *Nantwich*
B Hewitt, *ditto*
Dormer Harris, Esq. *ditto*
Mr. J. Higson, *Frodsham*
Hulley, *ditto*
S. Higginson, *Minshull*
C. Hindley, *Manchester*
R. Hindley, *ditto*
E. Holme *ditto*
Hall, *ditto*
Heywood, *ditto*
J. Heywood, *ditto*
T. Hudson *ditto*
Haughton, *ditto*
J. Hilton, *ditto*
J. Hall, *ditto*
Rev. Mr. Haughton, *ditto*
Mr. T. Henry, *ditto*
R. Harrison, *Salford*
Miss Harrison, *Manchester*
Rev. S. Hall, *ditto*
Mr. Hulse, *Bucklow-Hill*
R. Hodgkinson, *Prefect*
J. Hodgkinson, *ditto*
A. Hitchin, *Newton*

(5)

I.

—— Ince, Efq. *Chrifleton*, 2 copies
Mrs. Inman, *Sedberg*
Mrs. Jeffreys, *Northwich*
Rev. Mr. Croxton Johnfon, *Wilmflow*
Mr. Johnfon, *Congleton*
Mrs. Johnfon, *Nantwich*
Mr. P. Johnfon, *Davenham*
Rev. H. Jackfon, *Manchefter*
Mrs. M. Jackfon, *Middlewich*
Mr. Jackfon, *Chefter*
Jackfon, *Frodfham*
Jackfon, *Macclesfield*
Rev. Mr. Jennings, *Macclesfield*
Rev. Mr. Ingles, *ditto*
Mr. Joynfon, *Middlewich*
Mr. T. Jackfon, *Nunhoufe*
Mr. Jones, *Weaverham*
Mr. Jarvis, *Prefect*
J. Jarvis, *ditto*
Mr. T. Jones, *Charnock*
W. Jones, *Manchefter*
R. Johnfon, *Macclesfield*
Mrs. Jones, *Cheetham*
Mr. W. Johnfon, *Manchefter*

K.

Richard Kent, Efq. *Liverpool*
Rev. Mr. Kent, *Nantwich*
Rev. Mr. R. Kent, *Minfhull*
Mr. Kent, *Loftock*
Mr. Kent, *Knutsford*
Rev. Mr. Kitchen, *Liverpool*
Capt. Kinfey, *Knutsford*
Mr. W. Kinfey, *Swettenham*
Mr. Kay, *Knutsford*
Mifs Kirby, *Congleton*
Mr. Kennerley, *Swettenham*
M. S. Kennerley, *Middlewich*
Mrs. Kenyons, *Chefter*
Mr. Kenworthy, *Preftbury*
Mr. J. Kenworthy, *Manchefter*

L.

Sir John Fleming Leicefter, Bart. *Tabley*, 4 copies
Henry Cornwall Legh, Efq. *High-Legh*, 2 copies
G. Leycefter, Efq. *Toft*, 2 copies

Rev. Mr. Archdeacon Leigh, *Lyt*
John Leigh, Efq. *Oughtrington*,
John Leigh, Efq. *B. L. Chefter*,
Egerton Leigh, Efq. *Twemlow*
Mrs. Leigh
G. Lloyd, Efq. *Higher Tabley*
S. Langford, Efq. *Macclesfield*
H. Langford, Efq. *Stockport*
Mrs. Leeke, *Middlewich*
Mr. T. Leigh, jun. *Macclesfield*
J. Lean, *ditto*
J. Lomas, *ditto*
S. Leeke, *Chefter*
Lowndes, *ditto*
Lindfey, *ditto*
W. Lowndes, *Sandbach*
J. Lowndes, *Swettenham*
Rev. Mr. Littler, *Northwich*
Mr. H. Leicefter, *ditto*
Leech, *Knutsford*
J. C. Leigh, *Woodley*
W. Ledward, *Peover*
T. Leigh, *High-Leigh*
Lathbury, *Clive*
T. Lockett, *Brereton*
R. Lowe, *ditto*
J. Lockett, *Longport*
P. Leather, *Halmead*
E. Lowe, *Northwich*
R. Lawrence, *ditto*
Lowndes, *Congleton*
T. Locker, *ditto*
Mrs. Leigh, *Afhbourn*
Mr. W. Lowe, *Nantwich*
R. Lowe, *Middlewich*
E. Lowe, *Liverpool*
Rev. Mr. Lewin, *ditto*
Mr. J. Lea, *Kermincham*
Lord, *Manchefter*
C. Lawfon, A. M. *ditto*
Mrs. Linney, *ditto*
Mr. J. Littlewood, *Ardwick*

M.

Sir Henry Mainwaring, Bart. 2 copies
John Mort, Efq. *Northwich*, 2
Mr. J. Mort, *Liverpool*, 2 copies
Counfellor Manley
Mrs. Manley
Doctor Mofs, *Warrington*

(6)

Mrs. Manwaring, *Knutsford*
Mr. D. Middleton, *Blue-Slates*
C. Middleton, *Middlewich*
Moreland, *Sedberg*
Mrs. Moreland
Mr. Maclardie, *Macclesfield*
Mrs. Maclardie
Mr. A. Mills, *ditto*
Maddock, *ditto*
Manifold, *Northwich*
W. Massey, Esq. *Chester*
Rev. Mr. Markham, *ditto*
Rev. T. Mawdesley, *ditto*
Mrs. Massey, *ditto*
Rev. Mr. Mostyn, *Christleton*
Mr. J. Mirschamp, *Beverley*
Mr. J. Morris, *Lawton*
Mr. Mairs, *Great Budworth*
C. Morris, Esq. *Lymm*
Mr. S. Moulsdale, *Frodsham*
R. Myers, *Liverpool*
T. Manley, *ditto*
Rev. Mr. Monkhouse, *Prestbury*
Mr. Mellor, *Nantwich*
Mellor, *Leek*
T. Mather, *Macclesfield*
W. Mather, *Warrington*
J. Mather, *Oardsall*
J. Mostyn, *Manchester*
J. Macaulay, *ditto*
R. Mollineux, *Prescot*
Rev. Mr. Morgan, *Acton*
Mr. R. Marsh, *Nantwich*

N.

Doctor Norton, *Macclesfield*
Mr. Theophilus Norton, *Swettenham*
Mr. S. Newton, *Kerrincham*
J. Newton, *High Leigh*
Nangreave, *Manchester*
Norton, *ditto*
S. Norris, *ditto*
Rev. Mr. Nelson, *Chester*
Mr. T. Nixon, *Nantwich*

O.

Rev. Dr. Olliver, *Sedbergh*
Rev. Mr. Olliver, *Chester*
Rev. Mr. Owen, *Warrington*, 3 copies
Rev. Mr. Ogden *Macclesfield*
Mr. Oakes, *Stanthorn*
Ollier, *Prescot*

Mr. W. Oakes, *Middlewich*
Ormson, *Frodsham*
W. Owen, *Coventry*
Owen, *Northwich*
J. Ollier, *ditto*
Olivant, *Manchester*
J. Orme, *ditto*
T. Oulton, *ditto*
E. Oulton, *Middlewich*
Miss Oulton, *ditto*

P.

Right Honourable Lord Penrhyn, 2 copies
Thomas Patten, Esq. *Bank*
Doctor Patten, *Warrington*
Rev. Mr. Parker, *Chelford*, 2 copies
John Parr, Esq. *Liverpool*
N. M. Pattison, Esq. *Congleton*, 2 copies
Doctor Percival, F. R. S. *Manchester*
Rev. Mr. Powell, *Middlewich*
Mr. Parrott, *ditto*
Rev. Mr. Partridge, *Nantwich*
Mrs. Pownall, *ditto*
Mr. Richard Parry, *Llangollen*
Mr. Potter, *Manchester*
E. Place, *ditto*
Rev. Mr. Pedley, *Salford*
Mr. J. Pownal, *Manchester*
Preston, *ditto*
R. Parker, *ditto*
B. Potter, *ditto*
A. Patterson, *ditto*
T. Parsons, *ditto*
Rev. Emanuel Page, *Frodsham*
Mr. R. Parsons, *ditto*
M. Pemberton, *Warrington*
Rev. Mr. Pownall, *Warmingham*
Mr. Paddey *ditto*
Peters, *Knutsford*
Rev. Mr. Pollock, *Macclesfield*
Miss Pickering, *Somerford*
Mr. Pickering, *ditto*
Rev. Mr. Price, *Chester*
Mr. J. Pownall, *ditto*
Mrs. Phillips, *ditto*
Mr. Poole, *ditto*
J. Parry, *ditto*
J. Pierce, *ditto*
Rev. Mr. Perryn, *Standish*
Mrs. Peacock, *Great Budworth*
Mr. Palin, *Northwich*
L. P. Pidcock, *Buxton*
Mrs. Painter, *Uttoxeter*
Rev. Mr. Parsons, *Dedleston*

(7)

Mr. S. Potts, *Siddington*

Q.

Mr. T. Quincey, *Manchester*

R.

Bagot Reade, Efq. *Chester*
Mrs. Rawdon, *ditto*
Ravenscroft, *Davenham*
Miss Ravenscroft, *Newton*
Mrs. Richmond, *Liverpool*
Miss Robinson, *ditto*
Rev. G. Reade, *Over-Peover*
Mr. Roylance, *Winsford*
W. Robinson, *Stafford*
Ryan, *London*
D. Reed, *Northwich*, 2 copies
Reed
Rev. Mr. Richardson, *Chester*
Mr. Richardson, *Moulton*
Reece, *Hartford*
S. Rathbone, *Sandbach*
J. Rathbone, *ditto*
J. Ravenscroft, *Middlewich*
Ridings, *Manchester*
Ridgway, *ditto*
Royle, *ditto*
T. Rigg, *ditto*
Richardson, *ditto*
Mrs. Roe, *Macclesfield*, 2 copies
Mr. Rowson, *ditto*
Ryle, *ditto*
Reddish, *Prestbury*

S.

Thomas Slaughter, Efq. *Chester*
Hugh Speed, Efq. *ditto*
Peter Snow, Efq. *ditto*
Mrs. Swettenham, *Somerford*
Rev. Mr. Salmon, *Sandbach*
Rev. Mr. Sibson, *ditto*
Rev. Mr. Stringer, *Brereton*
Rev. Mr. Seeley, *Holmes-chapel*
Mr. J. Seaman, fen. *Middlewich*
J. Seaman, jun. *ditto*
Mrs. Sunderland
Rev. Mr. Sandford, *Manchester*
Mr. Serjeant, *ditto*
T. Stott, jun. *ditto*
Rev. Mr. Salter *ditto*
Mr. Shaw, *ditto*
J. Salisbury, *ditto*

Mr. J. Shuttleworth, *Manchester*
J. Seddon, *ditto*
Seddon, *ditto*
W. Steele, *ditto*
J. Smith, *ditto*
R. Shore, *ditto*
Rev. Mr. Sewell, *Prescot*
Mr. S. Southern, *ditto*
A. Stewart, *ditto*
C. Stockton, *Acton*
Rev. Mr. Sneyd, *Woolstanton*
Rev. Mr. Smith, *Nantwich*
Mr. J. W. Salmon, *ditto*
Skerratt *ditto*
Snelson *ditto*
T. Steele, *ditto*
Mrs. K. Skelhorn, *Knutsford*
Mr. Stringer, *ditto*
Miss E. Seller, *Chester*
Mr. S. Seller, *ditto*
J. Sellers, *ditto*
D. Smith, *ditto*
Sanders, *Burlington*
Rev. Mr. Steele, *Peover*
Mrs. Smith, *Congleton*
Mr. C. Skerratt, *ditto*
Schofield, *ditto*
W. Swinton, *Wheelock*
Rev. Mr. Shuttleworth, *Littleborough*
Mr. Shuttleworth, *Warrington*
T. Sutton, *Middlewich*
Rev. Mr. Smith, *Tarvin*
Mr. Smith, *Tetton*
Smith, *Uttoxeter*
J. Swindall, *Witton*
J. Stubbs, *ditto*
T. Saxon, *Northwich*
R. Sefton, *Alpraham*
Rev. Mr. Sharpe, *Macclesfield*
Rev. Mr. Simpson, *ditto*
Mr. S. Street, *ditto*
Swanwick, *ditto*
Mrs. Stone, *ditto*
Mr. J. Shaw, *Frodsham*
J. Seddon, *Acres Barn*
J. Shipley, *Somerford*

T.

James Tomkinson, Efq. *Dorfold*
H. Tomkinson, Efq. *Nantwich*
James Topping, Efq. *Whatcroft*
Mrs. Topping
P. Tarrant, Efq. *Chester*

(8)

G. Townshend, Esq, *Chester*
T. Townshend, Esq. *ditto*
Colonel Tucker, *ditto*
Mrs. Tucker
T. Taylor, Esq. *Lymm*
Mr. Thearsby, *Northwich*
Mrs. Tench, *Midalewich*
Miss Thompson, *ditto*
Mr. Twemlow, *Sandbach*
J Twiss, *Alsager*
Rev. Mr. Taylor, *Wrenbury*
Mr. R. Taylor, *Nantwich*
Mrs. Tapley, *Chester*
Miss Thweat, *ditto*
Mrs. Townshend, *Christleton*
Toplis, *Ashbourne*
Mr. S. Thompson, *Swettenham*
R. Tomlinson, *Liverpool*
R. Travers, jun. *Warrington*
Miss Travers, *ditto*

U.

S. Vernon, Esq. *Middlewich*
Mrs. Vernon
Miss Vernon
D. Vawdrey, Esq. *ditto*
Mrs. Upton, *Sedbergh*
Mr. Upton
Miss Upton
Rev. G. Vanbrugh, *Chester*, 3 copies
Mr. J. Vose, *Macclesfield*
G. A. Verch, *Manchester*
W. Vawdrey, *Swettenham*
W. Vawdrey, jun. *ditto*
P. Vawdrey, *ditto*

W.

Sir Peter Warburton, Bart. *Arley*
Thomas Willis, Esq. *Swettenham*, 5 copies.
Mrs. Willis
Mrs Wade, *Davenport-Hall*, 3 copies
William Barrry Wade, Esq. *ditto*
Rev. Mr Webb, *Ashbourn*, 6 copies
G. Wilbraham, Esq. *Delamere-Ledge*
Mrs. Wilbraham
Thomas Wilbraham, Esq. *London*
Charles White, Esq. F. R. S. *Manchester*
Thomas White M. D. *ditto*
William White, Esq. *ditto*
J. White, *ditto*
W. Whitehead, *ditto*
J. Whitaker, *ditto*
Miss Watson, *ditto*
Mr. J. Wright, *ditto*
J. Wright, *ditto*
Wheeler, *ditto*

Mrs. Williams, *Manchester*
Mr. T. W. Wilson, *ditto*
J. Wynne, *ditto*
W. Warren, *ditto*
Woodrooffe, *ditto*
Miss Eliza Wilmot, *Derby*
Mrs. Wells, *Sandbach*
Mr. Whitehead, *ditto*
T. Wickfted, Esq. *Nantwich*
Mr. R. Wickfted, *ditto*
Rev. J. Wilson, *ditto*
Mr. Wrench, *ditto*
C. Walker, *ditto*
J. Walker, *ditto*
Strethill Wright, *Knutsford*
Richard Wood, *Liverpool*
J. Whitlow, *ditto*
Willan, *Sedbergh*
J. Wilkinson, *London*
P. Wettenhall, *Bostock*
Rev. Mr. Whinfield, *Chester*, 2 copies
Mrs. Wrench, *ditto*
Mrs. Worthington, *ditto*
Mr. J. Cotton Worthington, *ditto*
Rev. Thomas Ward, *Neston*
Mrs. Williamson, *Congleton*
Williams, *ditto*
Mr. Whitfield, *ditto*
E. Walker, *ditto*
Wilkinson, *ditto*
Warburton, *Northwich*
J Warburton, *Winnington*
Walter Wilson, *Lymm*
Rev. J. Wood, *Altringham*
Mr. G. Worthington, *ditto*
J. Wrench, *Audley*
S. Welsby, *Acton*
Walker, *Over*
Whittingham, *Curtis-Hulme*
Whitlow, *Drakelow*
Whitlow, *Pickmere*
J. Wood, *Middlewich*
J. Waller, *ditto*
Rev. Thomas Webster, *Frodsham*
Rev. Mr. Watkin, *Barrow*
Miss White, *Birmingham*
Mr. G. Walker, *Salford*
Walker, *Macclesfield*
P. Wright, *ditto*
J. Waring, *Prescot*

Y.

Miss Yate, *Northwich*
Mr. William Yarwood, *ditto*
Mr. William Yoxall, *Nantwich*

The PURSUIT *of* PLEASURE,

In the OPPOSITE PATHS *of* VICE *and* VIRTUE;

Exemplified in the Characters of *Henry* and *Edward*.

HENRY, a youth, by Nature form'd to please,
  Possess'd of beauty, elegance and ease;
Was sprightly, sensible, good-natur'd, free;
And knew no want, for very rich was he:
Health bloom'd upon his cheek, but Pleasure's charms,
Tempted the youth to wanton in her arms.
Through Vanity's extensive wild he stray'd,
Dress'd gay, and each accomplishment display'd;

Nor doubted but his perfon, tafte and drefs,
Would to her temple gain him free accefs:
He fought her in the gay convivial round,
But fought in vain, for there fhe was not found;
A phantom, which affum'd her name and charms,
Danc'd in his view, and took him to her arms;
But poor and languid were his empty joys;
Remorfe fucceeds, and all his blifs deftroys.

His gay companions foon confpir'd to bring
The youth to laugh at ev'ry ferious thing;
To game till his eftate was almoft fpent;
His conftitution, next, to ruin went;
Reafon was loft in the inebriate bowl,
And paffion rul'd without the leaft controul:
Each fenfual appetite muft be obey'd;
While oaths profane his converfation fway'd:

Thus,

Thus, in intemperance, his days were spent;
His nights in lewdness, tho' 'twas Pleasure meant.

Those places where the gay and great resort,
Where Vice prevails, and Fashion keeps her court,
All knew him well;—his folly, too, was known,
And ev'ry gamester mark'd him for his own:
The tavern, play-house, bagnio, and the fair,
In his destruction claim'd an equal share.

Thus by a course of guilty joys undone,
His fortune dissipated, honour gone;
His constitution ruin'd by disease;
The wretched youth, his end approaching sees;
Sees the dread gulph, Eternity, appear
Open before him;—See! he starts with fear;
Unutterable woe, his looks express,
While black despair, his actions all confess;

In anguish, which no force of words can tell,
Nor pencil paint, he bids the world — FAREWELL.

———————

ON EDWARD's youthful form, the Graces smil'd,
While Virtue own'd him for her favourite child:
Instructed from his earliest years, to tread
The sacred paths, where Truth and Virtue lead:
Like HENRY, he was sensible and gay,
And Pleasure sought, but in a diff'rent way;
His fortune was not quite so large, 'tis true,
Yet he was rich, because his wants were few;
A pleasing independence he enjoy'd,
And was too wise to be the slave of Pride:
Strong were his passions, but by reason sway'd,
Religion's laws he never disobey'd;
Native benevolence possess'd his heart,
Of which, the smallest insect had a part;

He

He deem'd it cruelty extreme to hurt
A harmless bird;—nor did he think it sport
To chase the timid hare, or wily fox
O'er hills and vallies, woods, or craggy rocks:
Yet he amusements had, and not a few;
He shunn'd *false* pleasure, but possess'd the *true:*
O! with what rapture, Nature he explor'd!
What satisfaction did the view afford!
With Vegetation's curious progress charm'd,
The bright survey his grateful bosom warm'd;
Each plant, each flow'r, in elegance of dress,
Their great original at once confess;
The pleasing murmurs of each purling stream,
And lively verdure of the groves, the same:
The gay harmonious songsters of the wood,
In concert join'd, while EDWARD listening stood;
Not MARA's voice, nor BILLINGTON's sweet notes,
Cou'd be compar'd with their melodious throats.

From earth to heaven, he rais'd his wond'ring eyes,
And view'd the vaſt expanſe, with glad ſurpriſe;
Obſerv'd the planets, while the moon ſerene,
With ſtars encircled, form'd a ſplendid ſcene;
"Far more magnificent, yon arch," he cry'd,
"Than RANELAGH's gay dome, with all its pride."

At other times, as inclination ſway'd,
The microſcope another world difplay'd;
The air-pump yielded him extreme delight;
Thus Pleaſure with inſtruction he'd unite;
In rational amuſements ſpend his time,
While HENRY's life was one continued crime.

He learn'd from Books the knowledge of mankind,
The various powers that ſway the human mind;
But his chief ſtudy, and his greateſt care,
Was his own conduct by thoſe rules to ſquare,

He found recorded in each sacred page,
By modern author, or by ancient sage;
These serv'd to strengthen him in virtuous ways,
And crown with happiness his future days;
His leisure hours thus pleasingly employ'd,
EDWARD the balm of true content enjoy'd.

Of his small fortune, never too profuse,
A constant fund for charitable use
Was set apart;—for EDWARD never turn'd
The ear of deafness, when affliction mourn'd;
Oft to the orphan, he a parent prov'd,
Nor e'er cou'd see the widow's tears unmov'd;
Nor did the poor, his bounteous hand reliev'd,
Feel half that happiness, himself receiv'd.
O seize, ye affluent, this power to bless!
Earth has no joys, like comforting distress.

Tho'

Tho' EDWARD's foul by Virtue was poſſeſs'd,
Love was no ſtranger to his gentle breaſt;
He felt its animating force, for one
Who reign'd the miſtreſs of his heart alone;
In her, he found that excellence he ſought,
A mind like his, with ev'ry virtue fraught;
The bliſs of MILTON's wedded love he prov'd,
For life united to the fair he lov'd;
His joys ſhe ſhar'd, his ſorrows were her own,
Nor did he form a wiſh to her unknown;
Their children, by their bright example fir'd,
Trod in their paths, and were like them admir'd.

Thus EDWARD lives, reſpected and eſteem'd
By all who know him;—and a bleſſing deem'd
To ſuffering indigence; friend of mankind,
Forward he looks, nor caſts a wiſh behind;

The awful hour of his approaching fate,
He calmly fees, nor dreads a future ſtate;
But reſts in hope to quit his houſe of clay,
For the bright manſions of eternal day.

The NATURAL CHILD.

LET not the title of my verſe offend,
    Nor let the Prude contract her rigid brow;
That helpleſs Innocence demands a friend,
    Virtue herſelf will cheerfully allow:

And ſhou'd my pencil prove too weak to paint,
    The ills attendant on the babe ere born;
Whoſe parents ſwerv'd from Virtue's mild reſtraint,
    Forgive th' attempt, nor treat the Muſe with ſcorn.

Yon rural farm, where Mirth was wont to dwell,
    Of Melancholy, now appears the ſeat;
Solemn and ſilent as the hermit's cell—
    Say what, my muſe, has caus'd a change ſo great?

This hapleſs morn, an Infant firſt ſaw light,
    Whoſe innocence a better fate might claim,

Than to be shunn'd as hateful to the sight,
  And banish'd soon as it receives a name.

No joy attends its entrance into life,
  No smile upon its mother's face appears,
She cannot smile, alas! she is no wife;
  But vents the sorrows of her heart in tears.

No father flies to clasp it to his breast,
  And bless the pow'r that gave it to his arms;
To see his form, in miniature, express'd,
  Or trace, with ecstacy, its mother's charms.

Unhappy babe! thy father is thy foe!
  Oft shall he wish thee number'd with the dead;
His crime entails on thee a load of woe,
  And sorrow heaps on thy devoted head.

Torn from its mother's breaſt, by ſhame or pride,
   No matter which—to hireling hands aſſign'd;
A parent's tenderneſs, when thus deny'd,
   Can it be thought its nurſe is over-kind?

Too many, like this infant may we ſee,
   Expos'd, abandon'd, helpleſs and forlorn;
'Till death, misfortune's friend, has ſet them free,
   From a rude world, which gave them nought but ſcorn.

Too many mothers—horrid to relate!
   Soon as their infants breathe the vital air,
Deaf to their plaintive cries, their helpleſs ſtate,
   Led on by ſhame, and driv'n by deſpair,

Fell murderers become——Here ceaſe, my pen,
   And leave theſe wretched victims of deſpair;
But ah! what puniſhments await the men,
   Who, in ſuch depths of mis'ry, plunge the fair.

The MISER; a FABLE.

A MISER, thirsting after gain,
Had led a life of care and pain;
And, tho' his chests were cramm'd with gold,
Yet hunger, nakedness and cold,
Had quite worn out his meagre frame,
And death, in all his horrors came.

Food meet for worms, his carcase made,
One Penny in his mouth was laid,
His passage over Styx to pay,
As was the custom of that day;
His wealth, his glad relations shar'd;
Yet grudg'd the penny they had spar'd.

Soon on the banks of Styx, his shade
Arriv'd; where Charon's boat convey'd,

Those ghosts who paid the usual fare,
Across the lake, with special care;
While those, who nothing had to pay,
With Charon's oar were push'd away.
It griev'd the Miser to the heart,
With his dear penny thus to part;
To cheat the ferry-man, he try'd,
Plung'd in; and swam to th' other side.

Affrighted! Cerberus bark'd thrice,
Out rush'd the furies in a trice,
Seiz'd on the bold intruding shade,
And thence, to Minos' court convey'd
Him—there accus'd;—the judge long time
Spent, in examining the crime;
Likewise the punishment its due,
As being of a nature new.

Says he,—" What does this wretch deferve ?—
" Tantalus' torments will not ferve;
" Nor will the wheel of Ixion do—
" Shall he the rolling ftone purfue,
" With Sifyphus ?—or feel the pain
" Prometheus feels ?—or pour, in vain,
" Water, the fieve-like jar to fill,
" With thofe, who did their hufbands kill;
" Ægyptus' daughters ?—hateful crew ?
" Ah! no, thefe torments will not do,"

Stern Minos cries,—" But open wide yon door,
" I've greater punifhments than thefe in ftore—
" To rend his avaricious foul in twain,
" I'll fend him hence, to his own world again,
" His own eftate; to view his lavifh heirs,
" Wafting the produce of his toils and cares:
" A fight like *this*, the wretch himfelf fhall own,
" Exceeds each torment in thefe regions known."

A Specimen

A Specimen of MODERN FEMALE EDUCATION.

MARIA, from her infant years,
　　Was all her mother's hopes and fears;
To such a pitch that fondness grew,
Miss did—whate'er she chose to do;
Sole mistress of the nurs'ry, she
Indulg'd in ev'ry thing must be;
The maids, as order'd, still supply'd
Her wants, and trembl'd if she cry'd;
She must not cry, rather than that,
To pieces goes my Lady's hat;
Gauzes and ribbands form a broom,
And ostrich feathers sweep the room:
Nay, shou'd she feel a strong desire,
To see Sir Charles's wig on fire,
Rather than tears shou'd spoil her face,
Another soon supplies its place.

Under such government as this,
Can it be wonder'd at, that Miss
Soon grew above my Lady's hand,
Nor e'er wou'd brook a reprimand.

To Boarding-School she now was sent;
But, 'twas thought proper, e'er she went,
To give the Governess her cue,
And tell her what she had to do:
" Dear Mrs. Sage," my Lady cries,
" Pray don't let reading spoil her eyes,
" Nor needle-work; and, do ye hear;
" Be sure you take the greatest care,
" That none e'er contradicts my child,
" She can't bear *that*, she's been so spoil'd."

The Governess, in hopes to please
Her Ladyship, to this agrees;

Takes the young Lady with her home,
And gives her the genteeleſt room:
But ſhe, who ne'er had known reſtraint,
Soon gave occaſion for complaint;
Unruly, inſolent and vain,
She thought o'er all the ſchool to reign.

The Governeſs, to ſoothe her pride,
To reaſon with Maria try'd,
But all in vain, for, void of grace,
She ſlapp'd her Miſtreſs in the face.

My Lady heard the tale, and ſmil'd;
Admir'd the ſpirit of the child;
Hop'd ſhe'd excuſe it — but ſhe'd call
At ſchool, next day, and ſettle all.

Accordingly, next day ſhe goes,
To chide her daughter, you'll ſuppoſe;

Not an improbable conjecture,
She gave her—*a moſt trimming lecture.*

Says ſhe, " Maria, what I hear
" You've miſbehav'd ;—kiſs me, my dear ;
" Indeed it was not right to hit
(Then burſt into a laughing fit)
" Your Governeſs upon the face ;
" You ought to ſuffer ſome diſgrace
" For ſuch behaviour—nay, don't cry,
" I'll ſend you ſomething, by and by,
" A fine gold watch ; and ſee, what's here,
" Some pretty trinkets—take 'em dear,
" And give your Governeſs a kiſs—"
With much ado, the ſtubborn Miſs,
At length, conſented to be friends,
And *thus*, my Lady's chiding ends.

But 'tis not very hard to guefs,
How much *this* hurt her Governefs;
However, fhe agreed at laft,
No more to notice what had paft,
Provided Mifs, in future, wou'd
Be very tractable and good—
" Good!" cries my Lady, " to be fure!
" Have not I juft been talking to her?
" She'll be much better, without doubt—".
This pafs'd, as fhe was going out.

The fequel fhew'd, how much improv'd,
Mifs was, by being fo reprov'd;
For ere another day was o'er,
She lock'd her Miftrefs out of door.

This treatment rous'd the gentle dame,
And to avoid ftill greater fhame,

She

She sent her home, to her wise mother,
Who, when a child, was such another;
And shou'd Maria chance to wed,
Just so, her daughter must be bred.

If children thus, must have their way,
Time will the blessed fruit display,
And wives become, they run astray.

The OWL; a FABLE.

A YOUNG Owl who, Narcissus-like, chanc'd to survey
Himself, in a stream which he found by the way;
Was so pleas'd with his person, so charm'd with his air,
That the bright God of Day, as he thought, was less fair;
Nor did Cynthia, his goddess, chaste queen of the night,
In his own dear opinion, appear half so bright:
Thus proud of his charms, he began to set forth,
In this curious oration, his honour, and worth.

" How oft to the Graces, sweet incense I've burn'd!
" At my birth, Cytherea my person adorn'd;
" I was clad in her cestus—gay Cupids around,
" With their wanton wings fann'd me—and now I am found

" Of an age fit for Hymen, who doubtlefs will blefs,
" Such a fav'rite of Venus—he can do no lefs,
" With a numerous offspring of beauties, like me,
" Who fhall chaunt thro' the groves, of the vallies be free;
" For O! fhould the race of us Owls, be once loft,
" To produce fuch another, would Nature exhauft;
" And happy, thrice happy, that fair one will be,
" That fhall chance to obtain fuch a hufband as me."

The conceited young Owl, thus with vanity fir'd,
With the young royal Eaglet, an union defir'd;
And difpatches the Crow to the King of the Birds,
Who, not liking her errand, began to make words:
" What reception," fays fhe, " can I hope from the King,
" Should he vouchfafe to hear the propofals I bring?
" 'Tis a match quite unequal—tho' nothing to me;
" But as yet, light and darknefs, could never agree:

" You

" You know the fair Eaglet can gaze on the fun,
" While the dawn of the day you endeavour to fhun;
" If your eyes are too tender, Aurora to face,
" Think of Sol's fiercer rays, and avoid the difgrace."

Thus reafon'd his friend; but remonftrance was vain,
For the Owl in his error refolv'd to remain,
And again urg'd the Crow; who, to humour his pride,
Undertook the commiffion, threw reafon afide,
And appear'd at the court—where her bus'nefs made known,
She obtain'd firft a fmile, then this fpeech from the throne—
" If your Mafter expects an alliance with me,
" His fine face in the air, at mid-day, let me fee."

'Twas enough for the Owl, who prepar'd for the flight,
On the wings of Ambition, not dreading the light;
But foon, with the radiance of Phœbus ftruck blind,
His way thro' the air, he no longer could find;

Down

Down he funk to the earth—and his brother owls own
That they found him at night, in a quarry of ſtone.

If to ſhine in a ſphere that's above us we aim,
We may chance to encounter with nothing but ſhame:
Had the Owl, in ſome cavern, ſought out for a wife,
Tis a hundred to one he'd been happy for life.

The WORM and BUTTERFLY; a FABLE.

A BUTTERFLY, one morn in May,
   With rainbow-wings, alert and gay,
As he was flutt'ring on a tree
Of honey-fuckles, chanc'd to fee,
A crawling Worm, attempt, with pain,
The top of a fmall twig to gain:

"Poor reptile!" fays the Butterfly,
"How durft thou venture up fo high?—
"Methinks thou wert by far more fafe,
"When underneath yon cabbage-leaf."

  The felf-convicted Worm reply'd,
"My folly 'tis in vain to hide;

"By

" By sad experience *now* I find,
" These twigs, when beaten by the wind,
" Lash my poor sides—the sweet-brier too,
" Has almost pierc'd my body through;
" Besides, I ev'ry moment dread,
" Lest some bird, flying o'er my head,
" Should snatch me up;—ah! why did I
" Forsake my cabbage-leaf to die?—
" Under its shade, tho' more obscure.
" I liv'd—yet still I liv'd secure;
" And, if I must confess the truth,
" The cabbage better pleas'd my tooth,
" Than all the flow'rets now in bloom,
" Which shed around such sweet perfume;
" But by ambition vainly fir'd,
" To see the world I *thus* aspir'd."

Butterfly. What have you seen, friend, may I aſk,
To compenſate this toilſome taſk?—

Worm. Nothing, but that, go where I will,
I find myſelf a reptile ſtill;
And wonder, creatures ſuch as we,
The beams of Sol ſhould ever ſee:
O, had I wings like you, to fly
About, and baſk beneath his eye;
At pleaſure rove from flow'r to flow'r
To ſip the dew—and ſeek ſome bow'r
When darkneſs comes—O! for ſuch bliſs—
Who would not cheriſh life like this?—

Butterfly. Your 'plaints are juſt—but patience, friend,
Another year your woes may end;
For, tho' my tale be ſtrange, 'tis true,
Laſt winter I was ſuch as you;

A grov'ling

A grov'ling worm, depreſt and low;
Bound by the froſt, o'erwhelm'd with ſnow;
Wrapt in the garb myſelf had ſpun
Ere winter's icy reign begun;
And, but few ſuns have gilt the ſky,
Since I became a Butterfly.

The Worm confeſt the tale was ſtrange;
But, when aſſur'd that ſuch a change,
Himſelf, with reaſon, might expect,
He ſpoke—in words to this effect:

" Henceforth, contented with my ſtate,
" Patient, the happy change I'll wait,
" Rejoic'd to be a Worm, ſince I
" May one day ſhine a Butterfly."

The MOON; a FABLE.

THE seven Grecian sages,
 Whose wisdom fame has spread,
Throughout succeeding ages,
 At Athens, once, 'tis said,

Were met in consultation,
 And *this* their grand debate,
What wonder in creation,
 Might be esteem'd most great?

When one of high conceptions
 Above the rest, propos'd,
What met with some exceptions,
 Tho' none its truth oppos'd:

Th.' Aſtronomer's opinion,
  That ev'ry fixed ſtar,
Through heaven's wide dominion,
  Which ſeems ſo ſmall from far;

Is like our ſun in glory,
  With planets moving round,
Where, tho' moſt ſtrange the ſtory,
  Men, brutes, and plants abound.

A thought, thus all-inſpiring,
  Each breaſt with rapture fir'd;
And, Luna's orb admiring,
  They earneſtly deſir'd,

Great Jupiter's direction,
  A moſt amazing boon!

His guidance, and protection,
   To bear them to the Moon;

Three days for obſervation—
   They aſk'd, nor wiſh'd for more,
Thinking, by application,
   Its regions to explore,

Ere half that time was waſted;
   And promis'd to recite,
What joys above they taſted,
   What wonders charm'd their ſight.

Jove their petition granted,
   And, on a mountain's top,
The vehicle they wanted,
   Was quickly ſeen to drop:

Artists of reputation,
  They took, to paint each scene
Found worthy observation,
  And enter'd their machine.

Mid thousands of spectators,
  Assembl'd to admire,
These aerial navigators,
  To distant worlds aspire.

Soon, with a rapid motion,
  They soar aloft in air,
While birds, in wild commotion,
  Attend a flight so rare:

But, Jove's own eagle guiding
  Their wond'rous air-balloon,
Thro' num'rous dangers riding,
  At length, they reach'd the moon:

F   Where,

Where, for their sole reception,
   A palace was prepar'd,
Sumptuous, beyond conception—
   On golden pillars rear'd.

On down of swans reposing,
   With their strange journey tir'd,
They lay next morning dozing,
   'Till half the day expir'd.

A table, most inviting,
   Next met their ravish'd eyes,
And, hunger's call exciting,
   They all, with glad surprize,

Partook of the collation,
   'Twas most delicious fare;
And, under such temptation,
   What mortal cou'd forbear?—

Wines, rich as nectar, crowning
    Their elegant repast—
All cares, in pleasure drowning,
    The minutes flew too fast;

For night came, unexpected,
    Their chief design forgot,
And, no one place inspected,
    Save that delightful spot.

Soon as the rosy morning,
    Had usher'd in the day,
The distant hills adorning,
    With many a pleasing ray,

The travellers arising,
    Determin'd to pursue,
(All sensual joys despising)
    The scheme they had in view:

Their thoughts, on contemplation
   Were now entirely bent,
And that day's obfervation,
   Sure nothing cou'd prevent:

But, while they were concluding,
   What road was beft to take,
Some vifitors intruding,
   Their compliments to make,

Unhappily retarded,
   The bus'nefs of the day;
Wifdom was difregarded,
   And Pleafure bore the fway.

The Ladies charms enchanting,
   Thefe ftrangers from the earth;
No requifite was wanting,
   To furnifh them with mirth:

Lost, to all sense of duty,
   In gallantry and joy,
Our Grecians, slaves to Beauty,
   Another day employ.

Their neighbours, envious growing,
   Of such a joyous band,
Rude epithets bestowing,
   Rush'd in, with sword in hand;

And bred so great a riot,
   So much disturbance made,
That some, to purchase quiet,
   To justice were convey'd:

As th' next day was appointed,
   For hearing of the cause,
The Sages, unacquainted
   With Luna, or her laws,

Against their inclinations,
    The trial must attend;
And *thus* their observations
    Attain'd a final end;

For the three days expiring,
    So very *wisely* spent;
From Luna's sphere retiring,
    To Greece again they went.

On terra firma landing,
    The people all around,
With open mouths were standing—
    In silence most profound,

Expecting strange relations,
    Of what was heard and seen,
By seven such wise Grecians,
    Who at the Moon had been.

The Sages foon related,
   The whole of what they knew;
The ground was decorated
   With flow'rs, of diff'rent hue:

Birds, on the trees, were finging—
   They knew not of what kind;
And, for the flow'rets fpringing,
   Cou'd no defcription find.

Thus, ignorance confefling,
   In ev'ry place they came
They met contempt, depreffing,
   Difquietude and fhame.

THE APPLICATION.

SO with Mankind 'tis often found;
   They tread the world's fantaftic round;

Their Youth, in gaiety is spent;
When Manhood comes—then all intent
On bus'ness—they've no time to spend,
In thoughts about their latter end:
Age brings its cares;—Death follows soon,
And Life proves one short visit to the Moon.

The LINNET; a FABLE.

YOUNG Celia was beauteous, and blithe as the morn,
   On her cheek bloom'd the lilly and rose,
And sweet was her breath as the blossoming thorn,
   When, to hail spring returning it blows.

Her bosom, with love, and with tenderness glow'd,
   But her Linnet was all her delight;
On the sweet little warbler that love she bestow'd,
   And carest him from morning to night.

How oft wou'd she open the door of his cage,
   From which he enraptur'd wou'd fly,
And, perch'd on her hand, her attention engage,
   While her lover unheeded stood by!

Yet oft, the ingrate wou'd for Liberty pine,
   As he saw from her window the grove;
And oft wou'd he wish his companions to join,
   Again thro' the woodlands to rove.

Unreſtrain'd by his Miſtreſs, one Midſummer morn,
    When Phœbus illumin'd the eaſt,
He flew to ſome birds, who were perch'd on a thorn,
    And forſook his wont ſeat on her breaſt.

" Ungrateful deſerter!" cry'd Celia, " away,
    " And meet the reward of your crime;
" For ſhou'd you eſcape the keen ſportſman's ſurvey,
    " You'll die of Repentance in time.

" But ah! his departure I ever ſhall mourn,
    " He was all that was charming and ſweet;
" And ſhou'd the dear fugitive once more return,
    " He ſhall ſtill greater tenderneſs meet:

" But vain the ſuggeſtion!—for tho' he may fly,
    " More quick from a gun flies the ſhot;
" And, ſo num'rous the engines, prepar'd to deſtroy,
    " That death is moſt ſurely his lot."

                                                Thus,

Thus, with direful forebodings, was Celia oppreſt,
   His loſs often coſt her a tear;
While he, far away from his miſtreſs and reſt,
   Silly bird!—found deſtruction was near.

From a net, which was artfully ſpread to enſnare,
   He ſaw a poor bird get away,
And, at ſome little diſtance, a kite in the air,
   Apparently, eager of prey:

In deep conſternation, his monſtrous beak,
   With wonder a while he ſurvey'd,
Rejoic'd to eſcape it;—but found his miſtake,
   By his former vain notions betray'd.

Said he to himſelf, in diſconſolate ſtrain,
   " How happy, the ſtate I regret!
" Cou'd I my fair miſtreſs's fondneſs regain —
   " That fondneſs I ne'er can forget:

" I again

"I again fhou'd be fed by her delicate hand,
   "As three times I was yefterday,
"When fhe ftrok'd my fmooth feathers—and now here I ftand,
   "Neglected—to hunger a prey.

"Ah! Celia, your bofom with kindnefs replete,
   "Has been cruelly ftung by my flight,
"But I'll hafte to return, and abjure at your feet
   "My crime, and be bleft with your fight."

He fpoke—and, like light'ning, flew back to the fpot,
   Where his miftrefs receiv'd him with joy;
He is faithful, fhe loves him—thus happy his lot,
   He'll never more venture to fly.

Like this fimple Linnet, how oft may we fee,
   The fond youth, and the love-ftricken maid,
From their parents' embraces imprudently flee,
   By falfe notions of freedom betray'd!

The

The REVENGE;

FROM A FACT, ATTESTED BY THE SPANISH HISTORIANS.

'TWAS night—and darkness all around,
    Her sable curtain spread,
When Claudio sought—and seeking found,
    The mansions of the dead:

For having, in his own defence
    Slain his invet'rate foe,
Ere he cou'd prove his innocence,
    Elsewhere 'twas death to go.

A church's sacred portal gain'd,
    He lean'd against the door—
Surpriz'd!—the door on which he lean'd
    Flew open;—but what more

The wretched wanderer did affright,
    Within the hallow'd dome,

He saw a pale and glimmering light,
  As issuing from a tomb:

Yet still had courage to draw near,
  When, dreadful to behold!
He saw, what chill'd his heart with fear,
  What made his blood run cold—

A beauteous Lady, clad in white,
  With wild and frantic look,
Rose from the grave;—while, at the sight,
  His frame with horror shook:

Who stepping, with a threat'ning tone,
  And with a bloody knife,
To Claudio, almost turn'd to stone,
  Almost bereft of life;

Demanded, what had brought him there,
  At such an hour of night?

The tim'rous youth, benumb'd with fear,
   And thinking her a fprite,

The truth, without referve, confeft,
   And why he thither fled —
" Art thou, indeed, fo much diftreft?"
   The beauteous phantom faid.

" 'Tis true, thou'rt in my pow'r," fhe cry'd,
   " But fear no harm from me;
" I am — and own the deed with pride —
   " A murderer like thee.

" A Lady of a noble race,
   " By perjur'd man betray'd;
" And doom'd to mis'ry and difgrace,
   " Tho' late a fpotlefs maid.

" The wretch who won my virgin heart,
   " Soon triumph'd o'er my fame;

                                              " Acted

" Acted the treacherous villain's part,
 " And boasted of my shame.

" I hir'd a ruffian — had him slain —
 " But not with *that* content,
" Still greater vengeance to obtain,
 " I to the Sexton went;

" And purchas'd, with a purse of gold,
 " Permission to explore
" His grave; — and *here* that heart behold,
 " The perjur'd villain wore.

" From his vile breast, these hands have torn
 " This heart — Revenge how sweet!"
She said—and with a look of scorn,
 Stamp'd on it with her feet.

" Be this," she cry'd, " each traitor's doom
 " Who our weak sex betrays;"
Then turn'd—and sought the Convent's gloom,
 To end her wretched days.

BELLARIO.

BELLARIO *and* MIRANDA;

OR

SUICIDE PROVIDENTIALLY PREVENTED.

ERE the arch rebel Cromwell's ruthlefs hand,
   Had feiz'd, 'mong others, on Bellario's land;
Embolden'd by the wealth he then enjoy'd,
He fought the fair Miranda for his bride;
She own'd his worth, his loyalty approv'd,
And lov'd the youth—but knew not that fhe lov'd,
'Till dire misfortune round Bellario fpread
Her train of ills, and all his hopes were fled:
When grief had feiz'd his foul, and anxious care
Stamp'd on his brow the image of defpair,
'Twas *then* fhe dar'd a mutual flame confefs,
And gave her hand, to fnatch him from diftrefs.

Behold him now, to affluence reftor'd,
Peace, love and joy, attendants at his board;
Four fmiling prattlers, as their mother fair,
Heighten each joy, and foften ev'ry care;
The charms of friendfhip, once again he proves,
If thofe are friends adverfity removes;
While his fond heart, with gratitude o'erflows,
Since, to Miranda's love, fuch happinefs he owes.

But ah! how fleeting are all earthly joys,
When one rude ftorm of fate each blifs deftroys!
A bafe, defigning, artful villain came,
His views conceal'd by friendfhip's facred name;
Who play'd fo well the wily ferpent's part,
Twining around Bellario's honeft heart,
That he, (ah! fatal confidence!) agreed,
For this *pretended* friend, to do a deed,

That

That drove him from the heights of human blifs,
Upon the dreadful verge of that abyfs,
That execrable cave, that horrid cell,
Where ruin and defpair for ever dwell.

Bellario, gen'rous to a fault, believ'd
The wretch's artful tale, and was deceiv'd:
In fhort, he madly ventur'd to become
His furety for a moft enormous fum:
When this was done, with fpeed the villain fled;
Leaving Bellario, with his flight half dead.
What cou'd he do?—the fum was very great;
To pay it, wou'd have took his whole eftate.
His own imprudence, how did he arraign!
And, of his friend's ingratitude, complain!
Then, on his lips Miranda's name he found,
And gave a ftart—for death was in the found.

"Wretch!

"Wretch! that I am," he cry'd, "how shall I face
"Her I've o'erwhelm'd in mis'ry and disgrace?
"Shall she, who made me what I am — shall *she*
"Be told she's ruin'd — and be told by *me?*
"It cannot be — there's madness in the thought:
"Oh! what distress has this rash action brought
"On my sweet infants! — Can I live to see
"Them plung'd in want, and wretchedness, by me?
"Shall *I* be witness to their *cries for bread*;
"And, rotting in some jail, perchance be fed
"Myself, by *that* cold charity may give;
"Just what will serve, to make misfortune live?
"Scorn'd by the world — reproach'd by ev'ry friend —
"Distraction! — No — this hour my woes shall end."

Thus, sunk in misery, and lost to hope,
He charg'd a pistol — and secur'd a rope;

Either,

Either, as undetermin'd which to chuse;
Or, if one fail'd, that he might th' other use:
Then wrote, to tell the partner of his care,
The dreadful cause that urg'd him to despair;
And to the window turn'd, for one last view
Of his dear children, ere he bid adieu
To *them*, and *life* — he saw them in the court,
At play; and stood a while, to watch their sport;
When suddenly, as Providence decreed,
One fell upon its face — he saw it bleed,
And flew down stairs, with all a father's speed.

Miranda, startled with the noise he made,
Ran to his chamber — where she thought him laid
For rest upon the bed, as indispos'd;
But, what a scene was to her view expos'd!
A rope hung from the cieling; firmly ty'd;
A pistol, with a letter by its side,

Lay on the table—what all thefe fhou'd mean,
She rightly judg'd, the letter would explain:
But who can fpeak the anguifh of her mind,
When thus convinc'd Bellario had defign'd
Thefe inftruments to rid himfelf of life?
Shocking conviction to a tender wife!
Amaz'd! confounded! horror chill'd her blood,
And, like a monument of grief fhe ftood;
When, rafh Bellario, on felf-murder bent,
Return'd to execute his dire intent,
And found her *thus*—he blufh'd with confcious fhame—
While fhe another Niobe became,
And funk, diffolv'd in tears — but *here* the mufe,
Hopes fhe the Grecian painter's veil may ufe;
To hide the fcene fhe has not fkill to paint,
And wanting words to tell the foft complaint
Miranda utter'd — but let *this* fuffice,
Her woe-fraught reas'ning op'd Bellario's eyes;

His

His rash attempt like cowardice appear'd,
He now prepar'd to face the danger fear'd;
To pay the bond, credulity had made
His own, and turn his fortune into trade.

That gracious Providence which fav'd his life,
Prompted the gen'rous father of his wife,
To lend his aid to save him from distress;
Thus, as a Merchant, having great success,
To affluence and ease, once more, restor'd,
He liv'd to bless the goodness of the Lord.

The BATTLE of AGINCOURT.

FULL many a long and toilsome day,
    And many a weary night,
Had HENRY and his Soldiers paſt,
    In ſad and diſmal plight:—

Oppreſs'd with hunger, wet and cold,
    On nuts and roots they fed;
Still on they march'd, tho' for twelve days,
    No better food they had.

Bridges were broke to ſtop their courſe,
    Trees, 'croſs the roads were laid;
All which they patiently endur'd,
    Fatigu'd, but not diſmay'd:—

When, coming nigh to Agincourt,
  They found a numerous hoſt
Aſſembled to oppoſe their march,
  And drive them from their coaſt:

Which, when the royal Henry ſaw,
  He bade his horſemen light,
And the whole army kneeling down—
  Oh what a noble fight!

With eyes and hands to Heaven rais'd,
  Beſought the Lord of Might,
To yield his bleſſing on their arms,
  And aid them in the fight.

Now from the Gallic army came
  Three heralds to the King,
Who, from their haughty generals,
  Did a proud challenge bring;

In which, they battle offer'd him,
    But left *himself* to name
The time, and place when they shou'd meet—
    An answer, which became

Brittannia's chief, was soon return'd,
    By *English* heralds brought;
Expressive of his daring soul,
    With Spartan courage fraught.

He told them; " *He* a constant march
    " Had kept, of late, they knew;
" *Oft* had they incommoded him,
    " And might have *fought* him too:

" But, if a *gen'ral* battle was
    " By their late challenge meant,
" They'd find him in the open field,
    " Prepar'd for that event.

" That his chief care fhould always be,
  " Never to do a thing
" Unworthy his exalted rank,
  " Unworthy England's King.

" He did not mean to be the *firſt*
  " To ſtrike the hoſtile blow;
" But, if attack'd, they ſoon wou'd find,
  " He dar'd to face a foe.

" That *he* his march to Calais, was
  " Determin'd to purſue;
" And if to ſtop him they were bent,
  " Much miſchief might enſue:

" Therefore, he gave them *this* advice,
  " And meant it for their good—
" To give him way—nor let thoſe fields
  " Be ſtain'd with Chriſtian blood."

But, notwithstanding Henry's care,
And offers to restore
The town of Harfleur—wou'd they give
The thoughts of battle o'er:

Confiding in their mighty force,
They nam'd the fatal day,
Which, *on themselves*, destruction brought,
Confusion, and dismay.

And now, of battle sure, the King
Might ev'ry day be seen,
On horseback, clad in armour bright,
With countenance serene:

While his brave soldiers, to a man,
Resolv'd to stand their ground;
Altho' great disproportion was
Between the armies found.

A valiant

A valiant Welchman, David Gam,
    Who rode beside the King,
Was sent, the enemy to view,
    And *this* report did bring —

" Please you my liege, there's quite *enow*,
    " For us to kill and slay;
" *Enow*, to serve for prisoners,
    " *Enow*, to run away."

Indeed, the odds were very great,
    For Henry had not more,
At th' utmost, than ten thousand men,
    Who, much fatigue had bore;

Whereas, the French commanders brought,
    (As their own writers say)
Upwards of seven score thousand men,
    Into the field that day —

Besides, the French were fresh and gay,
    And always well supply'd
With food—while Britain's half-starv'd sons,
    Provisions were deny'd.

Proud of these vast advantages,
    And certain of success,
The English army to destroy,
    They thought of nothing less :—

Nay more—*this* conquest wou'd repair,
    Their *former* loss and shame;
When Poictiers, and Cressy's plains,
    With Gallic blood did stream.

And now, like many others, who
    Build castles in the air,
The French, most cruelly resolv'd
    No living soul to spare;

Save

Save Henry, and his gallant chiefs,
 Who shou'd their triumph grace;
And be to Paris captive led,
 Their honour to replace:—

Then, insolently vain, in scorn,
 They of the King demand,
What he wou'd for his ransom give?
 Who told 'em out of hand;

" He hop'd a few hours wou'd so far
 " Reduce the Gallic pride,
" That *France* alone shou'd have the care,
 " Due ransoms to provide."

Th' important morn approaching, brought
 These boasters to the field,
As, to an easy victory,
 Assur'd the King would yield:

But

But *he*, who knew their greateſt ſtrength,
    Muſt in their horſe confiſt,
Had artfully his archers plac'd,
    Their power to refiſt;

Defended by ſharp piles, or ſtakes,
    Near ſeven feet in length;
Which, as they cou'd at pleaſure move,
    Serv'd to increaſe their ſtrength:

Beſides, two hundred bowmen bold,
    All men of courage try'd;
He plac'd in a low meadow, where
    The buſhes wou'd them hide.

The army's flanks the woods ſecur'd,
    And guarded ev'ry way;
In one of which, a troop of horſe,
    By the King's orders, lay

In ambush—ready to attack,
   Whene'er the battle join'd,
The Gallic army in the rear,
   And harrafs them behind.

The van was by the Duke of York
   Led up—who had defir'd
That ftation, as moft dangerous,
   With love of glory fir'd.

In the main battle, did the King
   Moft gracefully advance;
Compleat in armour fhining bright;
   The Royal Arms of France,

With England's quarter'd on his fhield;
   A fplendid crown of gold,
Upon his glitt'ring helmet fhone,
   Wrought in th' imperial mold:

His horfe, in fumptuous trappings dreft,
   A noble fpirit warm'd;
Proud of the royal weight he bore,
   His ev'ry movement charm'd.

The royal ftandard was before
   The youthful King difplay'd,
And other banners with the wind,
   In warlike order play'd.

While, on the other fide, the French
   Did in three lines advance—
The Dukes of Orleans and Bourbon,
   And th' Conftable of France,

Led up the firft—the others were
   Commanded by the prime
And flow'r of French nobility;
   Who thought it not a time

To ſtay at home, when glory call'd;
    For, on that fatal day,
Except the Dauphin and the King,
    Few nobles kept away.

In order *thus* the armies ſtood,
    No ſignal *yet* had broke
The bands which held the dogs of war;
    When Henry thus beſpoke

His valiant ſoldiers—while his words
    And actions, *both* conſpire,
To raiſe their courage to a pitch
    Which *envy* ſhou'd admire—

" My lads," he cry'd, " ye now advance
    " To Honour's glorious field;
" Nor doubt I, but your valourous deeds,
    " Shall make the Gauls to yield:—

" For my part—England never shall

   " For *me* a ransom pay;

" Nor haughty Frenchman proudly boast,

   " *I* to *his sword* gave way:

" No!—Death or Victory be *my* fate!—

   " I see it will be *yours*,

" The fury sparkling in your eyes,

   " Britain's success insures.

" Amaz'd shall future ages stand,

   " When told, the sword, the lance,

" And bow, such wond'rous deeds perform'd,

   " Among the chief of France:

" Yet tho' these pow'rful instruments,

   " May serve to purchase fame;

" 'Tis God who gives the victory—

   " Be prais'd, his holy name.

" And fure, a Providence divine,
  " Is guardian of our fate;
" Angels, invifible, may fhield
  " Our heads, when dangers wait:

" For England's people on *this day*,
  " At this moſt awful hour,
" Do, as appointed, keep a Faſt, *
  " And pray th' Almighty power,

" To blefs our arms with victory,
  " Then why fhou'd we defpair?
" But rufh like lightning on our foes,
  " And death or glory fhare."—

He

---

* It is remarkable, that this battle happened on the very day obferved throughout England as a general Faſt, for the fuccefs of the Britifh arms.

He ceas'd—triumphant shouts were heard;
    Each soldier seem'd inspir'd;
Each caught a ray from Britain's sun,
    And were what they admir'd:—

" Lead on"—they cry'd—" to battle lead"—
    And tho' the King wou'd fain
Have kept his advantageous ground,
    He found 'twas all in vain:—

Then, leaping boldly from his horse,
    Resolving to partake
Of ev'ry danger with his men,
    He cry'd—" *Now* let us break

" Through th' army of our enemies,
    " On *this* propitious day;
" And, trusting to the aid of Heav'n,
    " Their arrogance repay."

At his command the ſtandards mov'd;
  The archers on the right
And left, advancing on the foe—
  An old experienced Knight,

Sir Thomas Erpingham by name,
  Who did a truncheon bear,
Firſt led the way—and ſignal gave,
  By throwing in the air

The truncheon which his hand contain'd,
  While the whole army gave
A ſhout—that ſeem'd to rend the ſkies,
  And pierce each rocky cave.—

Then did the archers in the van
  Begin, with all their might,
To uſe their bows—and, as their dreſs
  Was for that purpoſe light;

They

They with such strength and nimbleness,
  Their yard-long arrows sent;
So irresistible their force,
  They pierc'd where-e'er they went;

While the two hundred bow-men brave,
  In ambush, wonders wrought,
Their ev'ry arrow wing'd with death,
  A sure destruction brought—

A thousand Gallic horse, against
  The archers in the van,
Bravely advanc'd—but were so gall'd,
  That on they madly ran

In much disorder;—while the ranks
  Behind them, pressing sore,
(The files being closely straitened)
  On those which went before;

Order no more cou'd be obferv'd,
 Confufion reign'd around;
Their horfes, both with arrows pierc'd,
 And finking in the ground,

(Which chiefly did of mire confift)
 Outrageous foon became;
Each art, in vain, their riders us'd
 Their fteeds again to tame.

Soon as the archers faw the French
 Advance, with fury fraught,
They all behind their pointed piles
 Retir'd, as quick as thought:—

Where, cover'd both in front and flank,
 They fafe from danger ftood;
And faw their haughty enemies,
 Immerg'd in feas of blood.

Their horfes fpurr'd, rufh'd on the piles,
   (Each fharp as pointed fword)
With which their fhoulders, breafts, and fides,
   Moft mis'rably were gor'd:—

Some flounc'd, fome plung'd, fome on the fpikes
   Their frighted riders threw,
Where, cruelly impal'd, they hung—
   A fhocking fight to view!

Of dying, and of wounded men,
   How dreadful were the cries!
Their armour, clattering, as they fell,
   Made a moft hideous noife—

Still adding horror to the fcene;
   While, thro' the yielding air,
A tempeft black of arrows flew,
   O'erwhelming with defpair

The Gallic troops; no longer proof
    Againſt the Engliſh force;
On their main body, back they fell;
    Their laſt—and ſad reſource!

The archers ſaw their order broke;
    And, ere their ranks cou'd cloſe,
Each graſp'd the ſword and battle-axe,
    And flung away their bows—

Then, boldly ruſhing on the foe,
    A horrid fight enſu'd,
Which ended not, until the French
    Were routed, and ſubdu'd.

Mean time, the gallant Henry fought
    In front of all his men,
Againſt the *ſecond* Gallic line;
    (Which firm had ſtood, 'till then)

Not only, as their General;
  But was alike expos'd
To danger, with each private man;
  And foon, a band compos'd

Of eighteen Gallic gentlemen,
  All refolutely bent,
To take away his precious life,
  Approach'd—with *that* intent;

And, boldly daring, nigh the King
  So *very* clofely preft,
That one of them, with battle-axe,
  Struck him upon the creft;

But *this* rafh action coft them dear,
  For, on the *felf-fame* ground,
Meant to be ftain'd with royal blood,
  Themfelves a death-bed found.

There too—th' heroic David Gam
  Immortaliz'd his name;
Defending of his Prince—he fell;
  His kinsmen did the same.

Henry was sensible how much
  He to their service ow'd—
And, ere their eyes were sunk in death,
  Knighthood on them bestow'd:

'Twas all he cou'd—for still the fight
  Was vig'rously maintain'd;
And soon, another dreadful scene,
  His royal bosom pain'd:—

Struck down with battle-axes, lay
  Extended on the ground,
His valiant brother, Glocester's Duke,
  Deprest with many a wound;

But

But the brave King preferv'd his *life*,
    At th' hazard of his *own*;
While *two*, in armour like to *his*,
    Were kill'd—their names unknown.

The Englifh, by their glorious King
    Encourag'd—*now* broke thro'
The French battalions—when the horfe
    From ambufh, came in view;

And rufhing—with a mighty fhout,
    Attack'd them in the rear;
Thofe troops had yet good order kept,
    But *now* they fled for fear:

Seeing the two *firft* lines give way,
    They no refiftance made;
But Alenfon's courageous Duke
    A nobler foul difplay'd—

Soon as he saw the battle lost,
  To kill the King he try'd,
And pressing thro' the thickest fight,
  The royal hero spy'd:

" I am the Duke of Alenson"—
  He cry'd—" thy greatest foe"—
Then aim'd his sword at Henry's head,
  And struck a furious blow;

Which cleav'd the crown, his helmet's crest,
  But did no *farther* harm;
Altho' this bold attempt soon rais'd
  A great, and dire alarm,

And so far th' English Lion rous'd,
  That, instantly, he threw
The brave Alenson on the ground,
  And his two foll'wers slew.

But

But those who were about the King,
  Enrag'd! beyond all bounds!
Dispatch'd the enterprizing Duke,
  With many mortal wounds;

While Henry's gen'rous soul was pain'd;
  But vain was all his care!
Tho' he cry'd out, to *spare his life*,
  His *life* they wou'd not *spare*.

Full three hours did the battle last,
  And *dreadful* hours were *they!*
For many a noble Lord of France,
  Resign'd his breath *that* day.

And, tho' the English victors were,
  And *those* who were not slain,
Were pris'ners made—yet, Henry felt
  Compassion's tend'rest pain,

When

When he furvey'd the bloody field
   Next day, in paffing thro',
Where heaps of carcaffes were found,
   And blood in ftreams did flow.

Nor did he quit the horrid fcene,
   Without *due* rev'rence paid,
To *that* Almighty power, who had
   Such *vaft* diftinction made:

So far preferv'd his fubjects' lives,
   That *moft of them* remain'd;
And own'd the battle of Agincourt —
   Heaven, not *his arms*, had gain'd.

The LADY and the DOCTOR; an ANECDOTE.

A PHYSICIAN of eminence, some years ago,
    Was call'd *in*, to attend on a Lady of fashion,
Who had long been admir'd—and the toast of each Beau,
Tho' *now*, her funk features excited compassion.

The Doctor no sooner the Lady had ey'd,
    Than he begg'd—" She for once would his freedom forgive,
" If he stept, from the rules of good-breeding, aside,
    " To mention the terms upon which she might live."

" By all means"—cry'd the Lady—" for surely no word
    " A *Physician* may utter, shou'd e'er give offence;
" Punctilio, in illness, is always absurd,
    " And shews either Doctor, or Patient want sense."

                                     " Why

" Why then, my dear Lady, I cannot refist
　" Pronouncing this truth, like a plain honest man ;
" That if, in the use of white paint you persist,
　" No med'cine will *save* you, do *all* that I can."

You astonish me, Doctor! but, such is my case,
　That I may as well *die*, as leave *painting* alone ;
For, shou'd I appear with my *natural face*
　Amongst my acquaintance—I shou'd not be known.

From SELIMA *to* ACHMET, *an* EASTERN MONARCH;

ON THE RUIN OCCASIONED BY A LONG, THOUGH SUCCESSFUL WAR.

THOU first of Monarchs, and thou best of men,
  Accept the tribute of my artless pen;
An humble Shepherdess for pardon craves,
While *thus* her wont obscurity she leaves;
Embolden'd by his clemency alone,
To bend before the mighty Achmet's throne.

This remote corner of thy wide domain,
Has often felt the blessings of thy reign;
And *here* the great, the joyful news is spread,
That *thou*, the beauteous partner of thy bed,
Hast, from her late captivity, regain'd—
We hail thy happiness, with joy unfeign'd;
           O! may

O! may *that* happiness be still increas'd! —
We likewise hear, that a most sumptuous feast,
Is now preparing, by thy sole command,
To entertain the nobles of the land;
On whom thy treasures shall profusely flow;
Gold, pearls and diamonds, deck each costly show;
And, that for many days, Music's sweet voice,
Shall cheer their souls, and bid their hearts rejoice —
But, Achmet, are not *we*, as well as *they*,
Thy faithful servants? — let *us* then be gay:
Yet know — we ask not for thy purple *wine*,
Nor — at the want of *delicates* repine;
We need no *gold* — and *jewels* were not made
To be on *Shepherdesses breasts* display'd:
A *greater* boon we crave, more precious far —
Restore us what we've lost by cruel war;
Whose horrid devastation fills our plains,
(Once, the abode of happy nymphs and swains)

With

With childless fathers—while the widow's moan,
And orphan's tears, wou'd soften hearts of stone:
Here virgin brides lament their wretched state;
O, gen'rous Achmet!—*good*, as thou art *great*;
Of *thee*, we beg our lovers—for we know,
None, but the *gods*, or *thee*, can such a boon bestow;
Give us our sons, our husbands, and our sires;
Our deep distress thy royal aid requires.

O! cou'dst thou, Achmet, for a while lay down
The pomp of state, and burthen of a crown;
And, like a swain, in humble garb array'd,
Leave thy gay court—our rustic soil to tread,
Here wou'dst thou find true misery display'd;
But, since we ne'er can hope to see *that day*,
Let thy poor slave the piteous scene pourtray.

Behold yon venerable group of swains,
Driving their flocks, to water, o'er the plains;

Bending beneath a load of years and cares—
See, how they totter!—Mark their hoary hairs!—
Long had they liv'd in ease—from labour free,
'Till their stout sons were took to fight for *thee*;
To bleed for *thee*, their aged sires they left,
Of children, and of ease, at once bereft;
Achmet, 'twas cruel *war*, and thy *commands*,
That snatch'd *those crutches* from their feeble hands.

Mark next, those pretty babes, whose flaxen hair,
Is to th' hot sun, and beating rain, left bare;
Their little lips distain'd with berries rude,
Which, hapless fate! is now their only food;
Their father's bow no sustenance can yield,
Each *cot* forsaken for the *hostile field*.
Ah! pretty innocents, who *now* shall form
Your tender minds, or shield you from each storm?

From

From favage beafts—or from the poifon'd fruit,
And pluck each weed of vice ere it has root?
Or who fhall guide your heedlefs fteps the road,
That leads to Virtue's ever bleft abode?

See! Achmet, fee! that *fad* but *lovely* troop
Of virgins;— fee how the pale lillies droop!
No longer on their cheeks the rofe appears;
Their brilliant eyes are dimm'd with falling tears:—
For *them* no more, the choiceft flow'rs are pull'd;
No more for *them*, the mellow fruit is cull'd:—
All fad and gloomy *now* appear the groves
Through which, their fwains *once* fweetly breath'd their loves,
In foft perfuafive notes—now heard no more,
Since, from their home, accurfed war has bore
Each lover, and each bridegroom far away,
And left *thefe* comfortlefs—to grief a prey.

Once

Once more (if thou canst bear the sight) look where
A train of dames, more wretched still, appear;
These, Achmet, *these* were *once* the happy wives
Of worthy husbands—peaceful was their lives;
In wedded love, unmingled bliss they found;
And sweet Content sat smiling all around;
But *now*, O sad reverse! they're doom'd to feel
Far greater woes than language can reveal—
When, with the morn, the rising sun appears,
The glorious prospect aggravates their fears;
For, ere his setting beams the West shall gild,
Their kind protectors' blood may stain the field:
Oh! dreadful thought! what horrors dost thou bring!
What heart is proof against thy pow'rful sting?
The measure of our woe is nigh complete—
Help then, O Achmet! help, ere 'tis too late;
Give us our friends, while they are *thine* to give,
So shall thy name to future ages live;

Prosperity, again, shall bless our land—
Friendship and Love return at thy command;
To *thee*, our hearts, with gratitude we'll raise,
And children, yet unborn, shall sing thy praise;

How, " When fierce tyrants kindled guilty war,
" Achmet, tho' seated in triumphal car—
" Bade war, with its attending horrors, cease,
" And—in the height of Victory—made Peace."

On DUELLING.

YE furious Duellists, who, with the sword,
   Glory your private quarrels to decide,
To check each haughty look, or hasty word,
   Which hurts your vanity, or wounds your pride;

Listen a moment to my rustic rhymes;
   No fulsome sermon courts th' averted eye;
But a faint picture of the present times,
   Where *fashion* teaches mortals how to die.

Too oft the tidings of the day relate,
   How, in Hyde-Park, or some like fatal place,
A youth, by sword or pistol, met his fate;
   Taught, by *false honour*, thus to shun disgrace.

To meet the King of Terrors, void of fear,
    All pure and spotless should our manners be;
The saint, whose breast of ev'ry crime is clear,
    Trembles at his approach, and stern decree.

But mad the wretch, who dares encounter death,
    Thirsting for blood, his murd'rous weapon rais'd
Against another's life; and yield his breath,
    When guilt, infernal guilt, his soul has seiz'd.

The Greeks and Romans, who, by turns, subdu'd
    The world, and gave it laws; for courage fam'd,
Never destroy'd each other, nor imbru'd
    Their hands in blood, when war no more was nam'd.

And shall a nation, where the Arts refin'd,
    Where Genius, Sentiment, and Learning dwell,
Be to such wanton cruelty inclin'd?
    Forbid it Heav'n! and blast the views of Hell.

When wife Guftavus* Sweden's fceptre fway'd,
   To fuch a height this horrid practice rofe,
That through his army, Duelling was made
   The common method of chaftizing foes:

Till by a *juft*, tho' a *fevere decree*,
   The Monarch doom'd the firft that fhould offend,
To fuffer death, of whatfoe'er degree,
   Firmly refolv'd his edict to defend.

Soon after which a quarrel rofe between
   Two officers of rank, who knew the King—
Knew him inflexible; nor cou'd they fcreen
   Themfelves, beneath diftinction's gaudy wing.

But both agreed an audience to requeft,
   And beg the King's permiffion to decide
The fatal diff'rence, which their fouls poffeft,
   Like men of honour, and of courage try'd.

* Guftavus Adolphus.

The King comply'd with their requeſt; but blam'd
. Them much, for violating Nature's laws;
Yet promis'd, at the time and place they nam'd,
 Himſelf to ſee them terminate their cauſe.

The morn arriv'd; the King attended came
 By a ſmall body of his troops, who form'd
A circle round the combatants for fame,
 As though he meant to ſee the fight perform'd.

" Now fight," he cry'd, " 'till one of you be ſlain;"
 Then, turning to the Provoſt-Marſhall, ſaid,
" That *neither* of our *juſtice* ſhall complain,
 " Soon as *one* falls, ſtrike off the *other's* head."

Juſtly aſtoniſh'd, at their Sovereign's feet,
 Upon their bended knees the heroes fell;
Implor'd his pardon; he, in accents ſweet,
 Bade them embrace, and friends for ever dwell.

This

This both aſſented to, with thanks ſincere,
  And, ever after, link'd in friendſhip's chain;
They bleſs'd their gracious Sovereign's pious care,
  Nor did the King leſs satisfaction gain.

O! had ſuch ſalutary laws prevail'd
  Where Liffy rolls along its limpid ſtream,
O'Brien had not his ſad fate bewail'd,
  Nor his misfortune been the Muſe's theme.

Born in Hibernia, heir to wealth immenſe,
  O'Brien was in Dublin college bred;
Where his high birth, large fortune, and good ſenſe,
  In all amuſements render'd him the head.

Youths, of the firſt diſtinction, daily ſtrove
  In his eſteem to gain the higheſt place;
He, *too*, the charms of friendſhip wiſh'd to prove,
  And found a friend, adorn'd with ev'ry grace.

Butler,

Butler, of equal rank and age, poffeft
    One of the moft benevolent of hearts;
And, with fuperior underftanding bleft,
    He was, befides, efteem'd a youth of parts.

In *him* was all that fancy could devife,
    When the the heroes of romance pourtray'd;
Form'd to engage the heart, and charm the eyes,
    In all the pride of youthful bloom array'd:

With him a friendfhip, of the warmeft kind,
    O'Brien form'd;—ah! little did he think
Such a connection, with his kindred mind,
    Would ever lead him to deftruction's brink.

Each had a fifter, virtuous, young and fair,
    Their hearts in unifon together beat;
The fun ne'er rofe on a more beauteous pair,
    And Hymen promis'd happinefs compleat:

For each fond youth grew ardently in love
    With the sweet sister of his dearest friend;
Nor did the fair their lovers disapprove—
    The nuptial day was fix'd, their cares to end.

But ah! the eve of that much-wish'd-for day,
    The joyful youths imprudently agreed,
Amongst their friends to pass some hours away
    In social mirth; when, as ill fate decreed,

A simple argument arose, between
    Butler, and one whom he esteem'd his friend;
O'Brien thought *he** much too warm had been,
    And gently did the other's cause defend.

From slight debates what mischiefs may ensue!
    O'Brien saw the gathering storm arise;
Saw his lov'd Butler's fatal rage renew,
    Vindictive fury flashing from his eyes.

* Butler.

Quarrels of friends are always moſt ſevere;
    Butler's warm temper could not bear rebuke;
'Twas cutting—from a friend he held ſo dear—
    An injury too great to overlook.

On poor O'Brien's head a torrent pour'd,
    Of harſh invectives, and reproaches keen;
His heart was pierc'd—his placid temper ſour'd—
    Reaſon gave way, and paſſion took the rein:

Words produc'd words—at length the public lie,
    From Butler, ended this their dire diſpute;
No means now left, but one, to ſatisfy
    The phantom *honour*—ev'ry tongue was mute:—

In ſhort, a challenge paſt; and both agreed,
    Next morning, in the Phœnix Park, to meet;
Revenge was *now* their object—love muſt bleed—
    Friendſhip be ſacrific'd at honour's feet.

                        But,

But, when the hours of cool reflection came,
  And reason re-assum'd her vacant throne,
The wretched youths, o'erwhelm'd with grief and shame,
  Saw all their schemes of happiness o'erthrown.

Anger was gone—and love, once more, prevail'd;
  Friendship's all-powerful voice again was heard;
But ah! their fatal challenge was reveal'd,
  And tyrant custom honour's laws preferr'd.

The dreaded morn, replete with horrors, came;
  Each, with their seconds, their appointment kept:
One had a cold—the other glow'd with shame—
  And both—spite of their care to hide it—wept.

Trembling, they took their ground, and both cry'd "Fire,"
  Three several times—resolv'd to stand the shot;
Death was, to *both*, an object of desire,
  And how obtain'd, just then, it matter'd not.

The seconds, unconcern'd, the conflict view'd;
   And, all-unfeeling, mark'd each falling tear;
At length O'Brien's, with an accent rude,
   Cry'd out, " The fellows are o'ercome with fear."

This, in an instant, rous'd their sleeping ire;
   Both fir'd—and sad O'Brien liv'd, to tell
How, by his cruel hand, misfortune dire!
   His dearest friend, his much-lov'd Butler, fell.

When, to his destin'd bride, Maria, came
   The fatal tidings of her brother's death,
Convulsions seiz'd upon her tender frame,
   And the grim tyrant snatch'd her fleeting breath.

Charlotte no sooner heard the horrid tale,
   Than, in despair, her bridal robes she tore;
Her tortur'd intellects began to fail,
   And sense forsook her, to return no more.

But how O'Brien wept, and tore his hair!
　　His friend he'd murder'd, and his bride was dead—
His sister mad—life was not worth his care,
　　For ev'ry comfort was with Butler fled.

In this distress, on suicide intent,
　　A worthy prelate timely interpos'd;
Who try'd, by admonition, to prevent
　　The dreadful deed, to which he seem'd dispos'd.

Religion taught him to revere his God,
　　And to abhor his meditated crime:
Calmly submitting to affliction's rod,
　　He waited, patiently, the Scythe of Time.

www.ingramcontent.com/pod-product-compliance
Lightning Source LLC
Chambersburg PA
CBHW020134170426
43199CB00010B/737